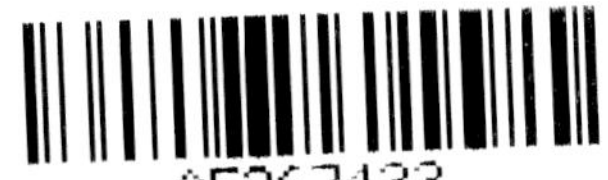

AF267422

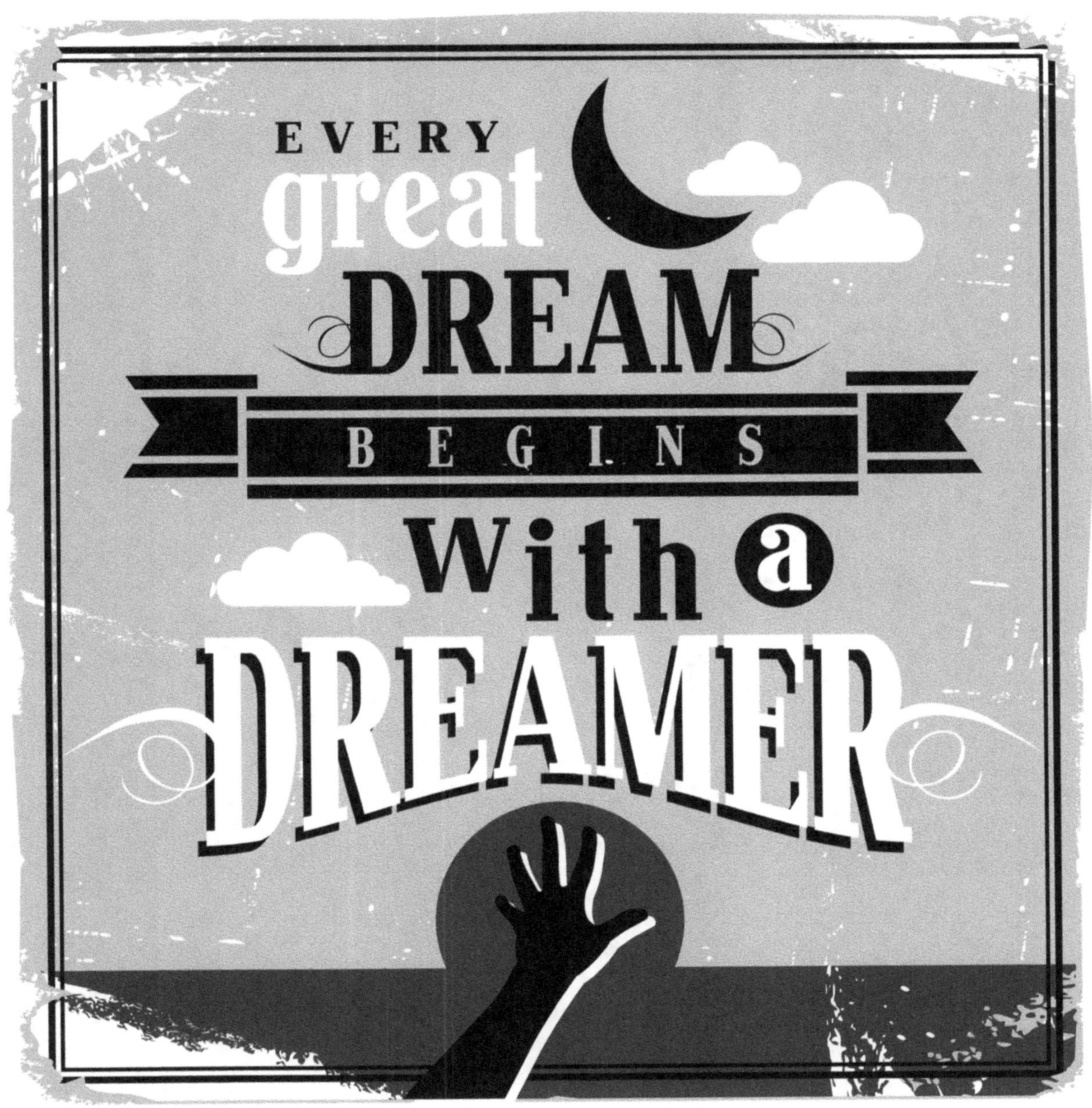

THIS SKETCHBOOK BELONGS TO:

____